AF228586

— OUTDOOR ADVENTURES —

HUNTING

By Tom Carpenter

SportsZone

An Imprint of Abdo Publishing
abdobooks.com

abdobooks.com

Published by Abdo Publishing, a division of ABDO, PO Box 398166, Minneapolis, Minnesota 55439. Copyright © 2020 by Abdo Consulting Group, Inc. International copyrights reserved in all countries. No part of this book may be reproduced in any form without written permission from the publisher. SportsZone™ is a trademark and logo of Abdo Publishing.

Printed in China
082019
012020

Cover Photo: Robert Nyholm/Shutterstock Images
Interior Photos: Andy Wak/Shutterstock Images, 5; Shutterstock Images, 6, 13, 14, 18, 21, 27, 32; Mike Mareen/Shutterstock Images, 8–9; Guilherme Mesquita/Shutterstock Images, 11; Szczepan Klejbu/Shutterstock Images, 17; Krystian Zalewski/Shutterstock Images, 23; Valentyn Volkov/Shutterstock Images, 24; Outdoor Media/Shutterstock Images, 28; Michal Durinik/Shutterstock Images, 31; Lux Blue/Shutterstock Images, 34; CLP Media/Shutterstock Images, 37; Julia Zara/Shutterstock Images, 38; iStockphoto, 41; Tom Tietz/Shutterstock Images, 43; Jeffrey B. Banke/Shutterstock Images, 44 (top left), 44 (top right), 44 (bottom left), 44 (bottom right)

Editor: Patrick Donnelly
Series Designer: Colleen McLaren

Library of Congress Control Number: 2019942087

Publisher's Cataloging-in-Publication Data

Names: Carpenter, Tom, author
Title: Hunting / by Tom Carpenter
Description: Minneapolis, Minnesota : Abdo Publishing, 2020 | Series: Outdoor adventures | Includes online resources and index
Identifiers: ISBN 9781532190506 (lib. bdg.) | ISBN 9781532176357 (ebook)
Subjects: LCSH: Hunting--Juvenile literature. | Recreational hunting--Juvenile literature. | Field sports--Juvenile literature. | Outdoor recreation--Juvenile literature. | Hunting guns--Juvenile literature.
Classification: DDC 799.2--dc23

TABLE OF
CONTENTS

CHAPTER 1

WHY WE HUNT

Thousands of stars twinkle overhead. Streaks of dawn brighten the eastern sky. A hunter walks along a trail through the woods. Soon she finds what she's looking for: an oak tree at a special spot.

The hunter climbs a ladder and sits down in a tree stand, a safe and sturdy platform. She buckles herself in with a safety harness.

As the sun rises, the woods come alive with nature. Cardinals and chickadees call. A fox scampers through the underbrush. Squirrels scurry among the frosty leaves.

But then a different kind of shuffling sound catches the hunter's ear. A white-tailed deer is walking through the woods. Will it come closer? The hunter

Sunrise is a beautiful time to be outdoors and a great time for hunting.

Venison can be prepared a variety of ways to provide a delicious meal.

raises her rifle slowly. It's a buck! The hunter's heart beats hard. She controls her breathing as she takes aim through the scope. Then she pulls the trigger.

Hunting is a natural part of being human. Thousands of years ago, people hunted to live. Hunting provided meat to eat.

Today, the reasons for hunting have changed a bit. Many still hunt for food. And hunting is an exciting pastime. But finding quality time to be with family and friends is another reason today's hunters enjoy the activity. So is getting outside and experiencing nature.

HEALTHY MEAT

Hunting is exciting. It is hard work. Most hunters say a successful hunt is just getting out and being in nature. But when a game bird or game animal is bagged, there is another reward: wild game meat.

The meat from deer, elk, pronghorns, and other hooved animals is called venison. Venison is red meat. It is a good source of lean protein. The meat from upland game birds such as pheasants, quail, and grouse may be white or dark. Ducks and geese have meat that is dark and rich.

RECREATION AND TRADITION

Hunting provides quality time away from home, work, or school. It also brings together family and friends. Many families go on annual hunting trips that

Few activities showcase the beauty of the natural world like hunting.

they look forward to all year. The experience itself is important. But packing and getting ready for a hunting trip are also fun. So is talking about the great memories afterward.

OUTSIDE TIME

Hunting allows people to spend time outdoors and experience fresh air, beautiful landscapes,

and nature. Almost all hunters will tell you they go hunting to "get away" as much as they do to shoot a game animal or bird.

Hunters can do more than hunt while they are in the field. Bird-watching is great. Studying wildflowers or prairie grass can be interesting. Listening to the breeze blow through the trees is calming. Watching sunrises and sunsets is relaxing.

CHAPTER 2

WHAT WE HUNT

Some hunters specialize in one kind of hunting. Others spend time hunting a wide variety of birds and wild game.

Most hunting seasons occur in the autumn. Fall can get busy for hunters. Good hunters know that the first step to hunting success is understanding the game they are hunting and the habitat it lives in.

SMALL GAME

Small game includes squirrels and rabbits. Gray squirrels live in thick woodlands. Fox squirrels are rust colored and prefer more open woods.

In the fall, squirrels eat acorns, nuts, wild fruit, and mushrooms in the forest and munch on grain from

Gray squirrels are a popular prey for small-game hunters.

nearby fields. Squirrels come out of their dens and nests as the sun comes up and spend the morning looking for food, either in the trees or on the ground. Squirrels get active again in the late afternoon.

Cottontail rabbits are popular to hunt. Good cottontail habitat is a mix of brushy thickets, grasslands, pastures, and crop fields. Rabbits spend their days hiding in brushy places and do most of their feeding at night, out in open spots.

BIG GAME

Big-game animals are challenging to hunt. Their keen senses—especially seeing, hearing, and smelling— alert them to danger.

White-tailed deer are found across much of the country. They like a habitat that is a mix, with thick cover for hiding and open spaces such as fields and meadows for feeding. White-tailed deer hide in dense cover by day and come out to feed at dawn and dusk. An adult white-tailed buck might weigh anywhere from 110 to 200 pounds (50 to 135 kg).

White-tailed deer are common throughout much of the United States.

Mule deer live in a variety of habitats in the American West. "Muleys" may live on the wide-open prairie, in mountain foothills, and in the mountains themselves. Mule deer are named after their big ears. An adult mule deer buck might weigh as much as 250 pounds (115 kg).

Elk are big and majestic. A Rocky Mountain bull elk typically weighs 500 to 800 pounds (230 to 360 kg) and has antlers on its head that can add

Black bears might be found near streams, hunting for their own food.

another 40 pounds (18 kg). Elk live mostly in the West, though more states in the Midwest and East have reintroduced elk and now hold hunting seasons for them.

Pronghorns live in the wide-open spaces of the West, where they can see danger coming for miles. Pronghorns are the fastest North American game animal of all. They can run up to 60 miles per hour (95 km/h). An adult pronghorn buck weighs between 100 and 125 pounds (45 to 55 kg).

Black bears are the most common bear to hunt. An average adult bruin weighs 200 to 600 pounds (90 to 270 kg). Bears are omnivores, meaning they have a diverse diet that includes meat, wild mushrooms, and plants such as berries, fruits, and grass.

UPLAND BIRDS

Upland birds live in a variety of habitats. That's what makes them so fun to hunt.

Colorful ring-necked pheasants do best in a mixed habitat of prairie grasslands, wetlands, thickets of brush, and farm fields. This gives the birds places to hide, feed, nest, and raise their young.

Elusive ruffed grouse live in the forest. But not just any forest. Ruffed grouse need young, dense stands of woods. Logging is good for grouse because it keeps woodlands young and thick.

WILD TURKEY

Four subspecies of wild turkey are common in the United States—eastern, Merriam's, Rio Grande, and the Osceola or Florida wild turkey.

Ideal wild turkey habitat is a mix of woodlands and farm fields, meadows, or prairies. Turkeys roost in trees at night and then spend the day feeding in open areas and woodlands. Turkeys eat acorns and nuts, tender leaves, shoots of grass, bugs, berries and fruits, and grain from farmers' fields.

Woodcocks are another woodland bird. Woodcocks like wet places where they use their long bills to probe for earthworms to eat.

Bobwhite quail live in the midwestern and southern states. Bobwhites like a mixed habitat that includes grasslands, grain fields, cow pastures, and brush thickets. Bobwhites live in coveys of up to 20 birds. They feed on small seeds, bugs, kernels of grains, and fruits and berries.

The prairie grouse family includes sharp-tailed grouse, prairie chickens, and sage grouse. These birds all need open habitat and prairie grass.

Colorful ring-necked pheasants stand out in the dry fall brush.

Well-managed ranchland makes a good habitat. Sage grouse need sagebrush. The bush's soft leaves are the bird's main food in the winter.

More mourning doves are shot than any other upland game bird—more than 16 million per year. Mourning doves like areas with grasslands, crop fields, ponds, and some trees.

WATERFOWL

Waterfowl includes ducks and geese. Male ducks are called drakes, while females are called hens. The two main types of ducks are puddle ducks and diving ducks.

Puddle ducks include mallards, pintails, wood ducks, gadwalls, wigeon, and teal. These ducks feed in shallow water by tipping their tails into the air and reaching their heads and bills down to grab the leaves and seeds of water plants. Some ducks feed on dry land in farmers' cut grain fields.

Diving ducks include canvasbacks, redheads, bluebills (scaup), and ringbills (ring-necked ducks). Diving ducks feed on plants in the water and roots near the bottom, as well as on freshwater shrimp, clams, and other organisms.

Canada geese are the most common kind of goose. Geese inhabit ponds, river backwaters, and open wetlands. The birds fly to open places such as fields of grain or greens to feed.

CHAPTER 3

HUNTING GEAR

Different kinds of hunting require specialized equipment for pursuing that type of game. For example, some duck hunters use decoys to attract real ducks. Turkey hunters often use calls to make turkey sounds and attract birds. Deer hunters might rattle antlers together to get curious bucks to approach.

But every kind of hunting has some equipment in common. Hunters need a tool (rifle, shotgun, or archery gear) to shoot game. All hunters need good clothes and boots to withstand weather and the elements. Certain accessories are important too.

Hunters have a variety of equipment to choose from, depending on the type of hunting they do.

21

RIFLES

All rifles shoot a single projectile or bullet through the barrel. The barrel is rifled. That means it has twisted grooves that send the bullet spinning as it flies out of the barrel and keeps going. That spin helps the bullet travel farther.

Rifles are loaded with cartridges. The bullet itself is the upper part of the cartridge. The lower part of the cartridge is the casing. It contains the gunpowder. A primer ignites the powder when the trigger is pulled.

Many big-game hunters use center-fire rifles. Small-game hunters often use rimfire .22-caliber firearms. Center-fire and rimfire refer to the spot on the cartridge that is struck by the rifle's firing pin. Caliber is the size cartridge a rifle shoots. Common calibers include the .243, .270, .30/06, 6 mm, and 7 mm.

The rifle action removes the empty cartridge from the chamber and moves a new cartridge in. The most

A riflescope can help hunters get a better look at their prey.

common rifle actions are bolt action, semiautomatic, and lever action.

Many rifles are mounted with riflescopes. A scope can help the hunter aim accurately.

SHOTGUNS

Bird hunters use shotguns. Shotgun size is measured in gauge. The bigger the number, the smaller the gun. A 12-gauge is bigger than a 16-gauge, which

Shotgun shells come in a variety of sizes.

is bigger than a 20-gauge, which is bigger than a 28-gauge.

Shotguns use shotshells. A shotshell contains gunpowder, a "wad" that separates the gunpowder from the shot, and shot itself. Shot, sometimes called BBs, spread out after leaving the barrel so that the hunter has a better chance of hitting a fast-flying target.

With shot size, the bigger the number, the smaller the BBs. Size 7 1/2 is good for quail, grouse, and doves. Sizes 4 through 6 are good for pheasants.

Most shot is made of lead. But duck and goose hunters must use shot made from steel or other nontoxic materials. Lead that would otherwise fall into the water might be eaten by ducks and other birds and poison them.

BOWHUNTING GEAR

Archery means shooting with a bow and arrow. Bowhunting is challenging because the hunter has to get close to the game to make the shot. Archery gear is broken into three types—traditional bows, compound bows, and crossbows.

Traditional archery gear includes longbows and recurve bows. A longbow is a basic stick-and-string setup. A recurve bow curves back on itself at either end, which helps the bow launch arrows faster and farther than a comparable longbow. Wood arrows are common with traditional archery gear.

Modern compound bows shoot arrows much faster than traditional bows. A compound bow uses a system of pulleys and wheels to make it easier to draw the arrow. They also let the hunter hold the string back longer before releasing the arrow. Carbon arrows are usually used with compound bows.

Crossbows shoot fastest and farthest of all, and they are accurate to ranges of 50 yards (45 m) or more. A crossbow is held much like a rifle, but there are powerful bow limbs mounted on top. The bow part is cranked back with a tool and cocked into place. The hunter pulls a trigger to shoot. Crossbows shoot bolts, which are similar to arrows but shorter.

No matter what kind of archery gear is used, hunting arrows and bolts are tipped with broadheads. A broadhead is a sharp, bladed tip that will bring down an animal quickly and humanely.

CLOTHES AND BOOTS

Hunters wear specialized clothes to keep them comfortable in different weather conditions.

Compound bows are popular with some hunters.

Much hunting is done when the weather is cool to cold and sometimes wet. One secret hunters use to help them stay warm is dressing in layers. The layers trap body heat, but a layer or two can easily be removed if conditions warm up.

Soft, quiet clothing is important for bowhunters and big-game hunters. Upland bird hunters need sturdy outer clothes to fend off briars and thorns.

Duck hunters are often around marshes and water, so clothing that is both waterproof and warm is vital.

Camouflage patterns on jackets, pants, and hats help hunters hide from game. During some hunting seasons, blaze-orange clothing is required so that hunters are visible to each other.

Good boots are extremely important for any hunter. Feet get cold easily, so warm boots are needed for hunting in cold weather, especially when the hunter is not moving a lot. Hunters who walk a lot need sturdy, comfortable, hiking-style boots.

ESSENTIAL ACCESSORIES

Each type of hunting has its own list of accessories, but there are a few items that almost all hunters need. Binoculars magnify the hunter's view of the habitat and help him or her see more game. Headlamps are important for hunters who head out in the dark to get to their hunting spot before sunrise. Hunters should carry a knife along with them. A multitool is also good to have for fixing other equipment or unjamming a shotgun or rifle. Finally, all hunters need to carry their hunting licenses at all times.

FIELD DRESSING AND MEAT CARE

One of the biggest rewards of a successful hunt is good meat to eat. But to have good meat, the game bird or animal needs to be field dressed properly. Field dressing is removing the animal's entrails and, in the case of small game, its skin or feathers.

A sharp knife and game shears are important for dressing small game and game birds. Big-game hunters need a good field knife to dress game in the field. If the weather is warm, a cheesecloth sack will protect the carcass from flies. Back at home or camp, a skinning knife helps remove the skin, and a good fillet knife removes meat from the carcass.

CHAPTER 4

HOW TO HUNT

Each kind of hunting is different. Successful hunters use techniques geared to the type of game they're hunting.

SMALL GAME

Squirrels are hunted in the forest. Woods with oak trees and acorns, and nut trees such as hickories and walnuts, are especially good. One strategy is to sneak slowly from tree to tree, waiting at each tree while looking for squirrels. Leaning against the tree to shoot helps the hunter get a steady shot.

Rabbits live in thick, brushy or grassy habitats where they can hide from predators. A hunter can walk through the brush or grass and try to scare the rabbits into running. Some hunters like to sneak along

Small game such as rabbits seek cover in thick, brushy habitats.

Some hunters like to stalk their prey on foot.

slowly and look for rabbits sitting. Hunting dogs such as beagles can help track them too.

BIG GAME

Hunters can choose one of three ways to hunt big game such as deer and elk. In stand hunting, hunters wait for game to come to them. Stalking is used when a hunter spots game in the distance and tries to sneak into position for a shot. Still hunting is slowly walking through an area and looking for game on the move.

White-tailed deer hunters often put up tree stands. They provide a better view of the habitat and help hide the hunter's scent from the deer. On the ground, hunters can hide in a blind. A ground blind gives a hunter a spot to hide in and wait for deer if there are no natural hiding places such as big tree trunks or brush piles.

Spot-and-stalk hunting can be exciting. First, a hunter gets to high ground or a tree stand and uses binoculars or spotting scopes to find game to stalk, or follow on foot. Before heading out, the hunter plans a route. Pronghorn hunting, which is done in open and often rolling or hilly country, is often classic spot-and-stalk hunting, but mule deer and elk are often hunted this way too.

Still hunting works best in thicker cover. The hunter inches along slowly, waiting more than walking, and looking for game.

A covey of quail take flight over a dry meadow.

UPLAND BIRDS

Ring-necked pheasants are found in areas mixed with farmland, prairie grass, wetlands, and brushy spots. Hunters can walk through these areas and flush out birds that might be hiding. Sometimes pheasant hunters team up with each other to cover more territory. But some hunters live for the challenge of hunting ringnecks one-on-one with just their dogs.

Quail live in coveys or groups of eight to 20 birds. They like a mix of grassy places, small grain crop fields, and thick brush. Finding these habitat features close together and walking a lot are key to quail-hunting success.

Ruffed grouse live in young woods with small trees and often next to wetlands. It's hard walking through these spots. Prairie grouse include sharp-tailed grouse, prairie chickens, and sage grouse. These birds usually live in open grasslands. It can take many miles of walking to find a bird or a covey of them. Dove hunters usually sit still on stools next to ponds or feeding areas and shoot at doves as they fly past.

Most upland bird hunters use a hunting dog to help find birds. When a dog finds the bird, the bird flushes into the air and the hunter shoots. Some dogs even retrieve the dead bird and bring it back to the hunter.

WATERFOWL

There are four good ways to hunt ducks: hunting over decoys, jump shooting, float hunting, and field hunting.

In decoy hunting, hunters set decoys out at a good spot on the water. Then they hide nearby in cattails, reeds, brush, or a blind and call to live ducks to get them to fly toward the setup.

In jump shooting, hunters sneak to spots that might hold ducks—a small pond, a little pothole, a creek, or a watery ditch, for example. Then they surprise the ducks and try to shoot one when they flush.

Float hunting is an adventure for two hunters in a canoe or small boat. They float in a stream, hoping to get close enough for a shot when the ducks flush. One hunter steers from the back of the vessel while the other hunter is in front ready to shoot.

Some ducks, such as mallards, wood ducks, or gadwalls, can be found on land. They feed in harvested grain fields. The hunters set out special

decoys that look like walking ducks. The hunters hide in ground blinds called layout blinds and call to hungry ducks that might come in for a look.

HUNTING DOGS

Hunting dogs are part of most kinds of bird hunting, as well as some small-game hunting. Many hunters who have dogs say that working with their dogs is the reason they hunt.

Flushers include breeds such as cocker spaniels, springer spaniels, and Boykin spaniels. Flushers find birds and flush them up into the air.

Pointing breeds include English pointers, Brittanys, Epagneul Bretons, German shorthairs and wirehairs, and setters. When a pointer finds a bird, the dog "locks up" stock-still near the bird and waits for the hunter to walk over and flush the bird.

Retrievers include Labradors, Chesapeakes, and goldens. Retrievers sit and wait with waterfowl hunters, then do the job of bringing back shot ducks. But retrievers can also be used in the uplands to flush and retrieve birds.

Hound dog breeds include beagles and Bassets. These dogs trail rabbits and push them back toward waiting hunters. Bigger hounds such as coonhounds, blueticks, and redbones hunt raccoons. These dogs push raccoons up into a tree after a long chase, usually at night.

Hunting dogs can help flush prey or retrieve waterfowl that have been shot.

CHAPTER 5

HUNTING SAFETY

Despite the dangers that go with any activity that involves guns, statistics show that hunting actually is a relatively safe activity. That's in part because hunters are trained to be conscious of safety rules.

Each type of hunting has its own special rules. For example, duck hunters on water should wear life jackets. And upland bird hunters should only shoot at birds in the air to avoid shooting other hunters. But one set of strict safety rules applies to all hunters.

Wearing orange clothing helps hunters stand out.

TAB-K FOR FIREARMS

Safety is important whenever firearms are part of the hunt. There are many rules to follow for firearms safety in the field, but one of the simplest and most effective plans hunters follow is known as TAB-K:

- **T**reat every firearm as if it were loaded. At all times.

- **A**lways point the muzzle in a safe direction. Always.

- **B**e sure of the target and what is beyond it. Every time.

- **K**eep fingers outside of the trigger guard until ready to shoot. No exceptions.

BOWHUNTING SAFETY

Hunters who use archery gear need to follow important safety rules too. In addition to being sure of their target and what is beyond it, bowhunters must follow these rules:

- Never walk with an arrow nocked onto the bowstring.

- Never nock an arrow, even when waiting in a blind or tree stand, until you are ready to actually shoot at game.

- Use a covered arrow quiver to house razor-sharp broadheads.

- Check equipment often, especially bowstrings and cables, to make sure everything is in good working order.

—TREE STAND SAFETY—

Because they involve heights and possible falls, tree stands can be especially dangerous. Here are some of the tree stand safety rules that hunters should follow.

Always have at least three points of contact—such as two hands and a foot—when climbing into a tree stand.

Wear a lifeline that tethers you to the tree as you climb.

Haul up gear (including unloaded firearms) with a haul line.

Wear a full-body harness in the stand to prevent falls.

Hunting serves many important purposes in society today. Many are practical, such as providing food and managing wild animal populations. Others are more sentimental, such as getting to spend time with family and friends and enjoying nature. It's a tradition that will continue to be passed from one generation to the next for years to come.

GLOSSARY

bruin
Another name for a bear.

buck
A male deer.

bull
A male elk.

camouflage
A pattern on clothing that resembles natural surroundings and helps hide a hunter.

center-fire
A type of ammunition that is activated when a gun's firing pin strikes the center of the cartridge's base.

conservation
The smart use of natural resources to help wildlife populations thrive.

covey
A small flock of birds.

decoy
An imitation bird or animal that a hunter places to attract game.

flush
When a game bird takes off and flies.

gobbler
A male turkey.

habitat
The area where wild game lives.

rimfire
A type of ammunition that is activated when a gun's firing pin strikes the rim of the cartridge's base.

tree stand
An elevated platform in a tree, where a hunter waits for game.

MORE INFORMATION

BOOKS

Alkire, Jessie. *Poaching*. Minneapolis, MN: Abdo, 2018.

Gurtler, Janet. *Small Game*. New York: AV2 by Weigl, 2018.

McNeice, Connie-Lee. *Big Game*. New York: AV2 by Weigl, 2018.

ONLINE RESOURCES

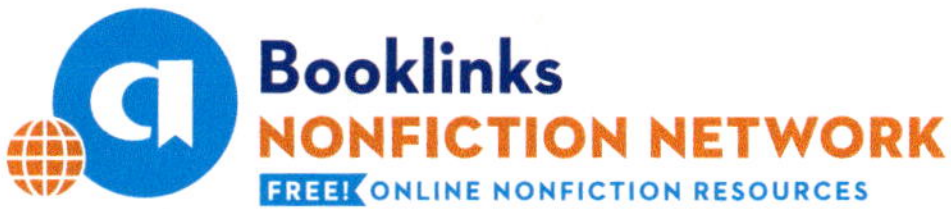

To learn more about hunting, please visit **abdobooklinks.com** or scan this QR code. These links are routinely monitored and updated to provide the most current information available.

INDEX

ABOUT THE AUTHOR

Tom Carpenter is a father, a sportsman, and an outdoor writer. He has introduced many children, including his three sons, to the thrills and rewards of hunting. A native of Wisconsin who always has part of his heart in South Dakota, he planted roots in the middle. He lives with his hunting dog, Lark, near the shores of Bass Lake, Minnesota.